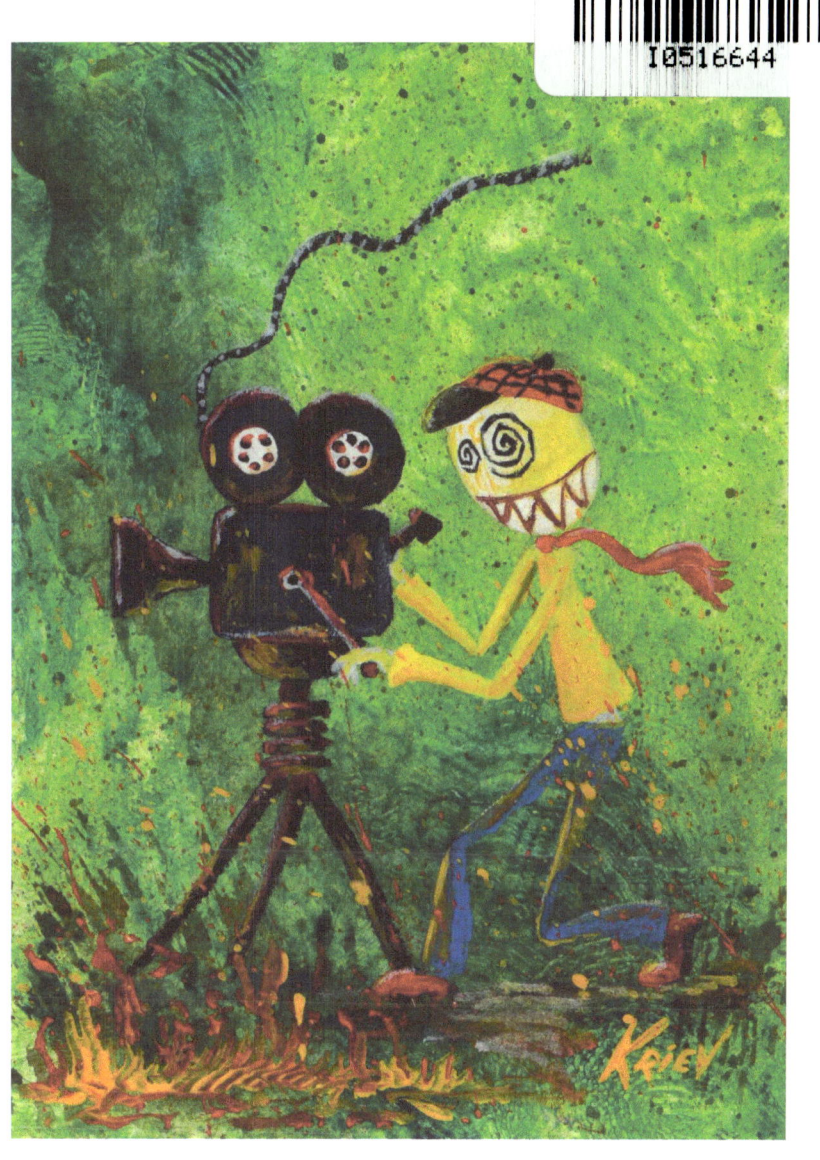

Making Movies

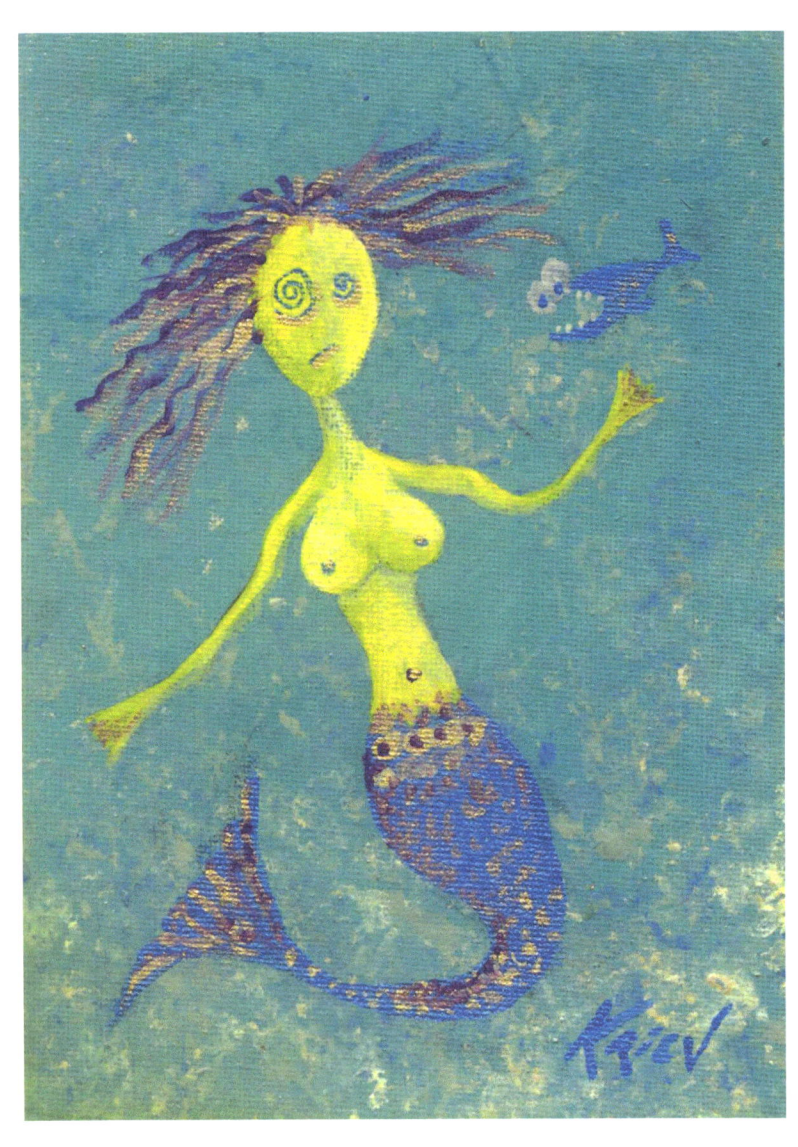

Fishy Lucy

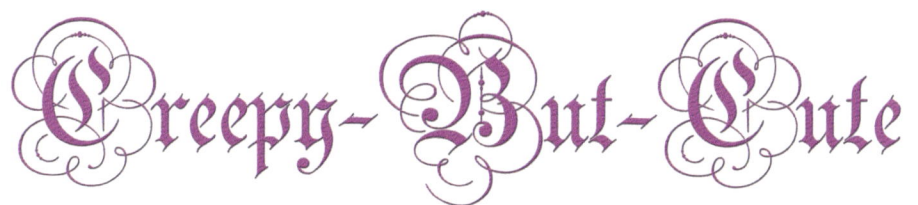

Creepy-But-Cute

Kriev is a child. Well, not exactly - but he expresses his psyche like a child would. His paintings convey unbridled emotions and impetuous feelings unspoiled by the vicissitudes of adulthood. His style appears unfettered by the rigor of the beaux-arts. The bright colors often reflect the joyous and carefree sensitivity of youth. However, the apparently innocent themes are often tainted with melancholia. The depiction of children with a wistful stitched-lip smile and vacuous eyes may be unsettling to the casual beholder. But behind this Gothic façade, compassion and tenderness are often present. So, as creepy as these little paintings may seem, they are, above all, meant to be cute.

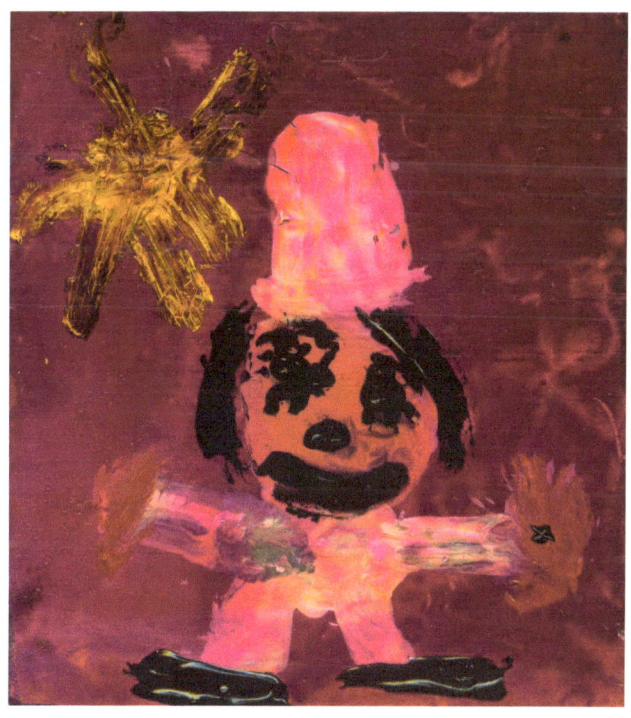

Self-Portrait - Age 5

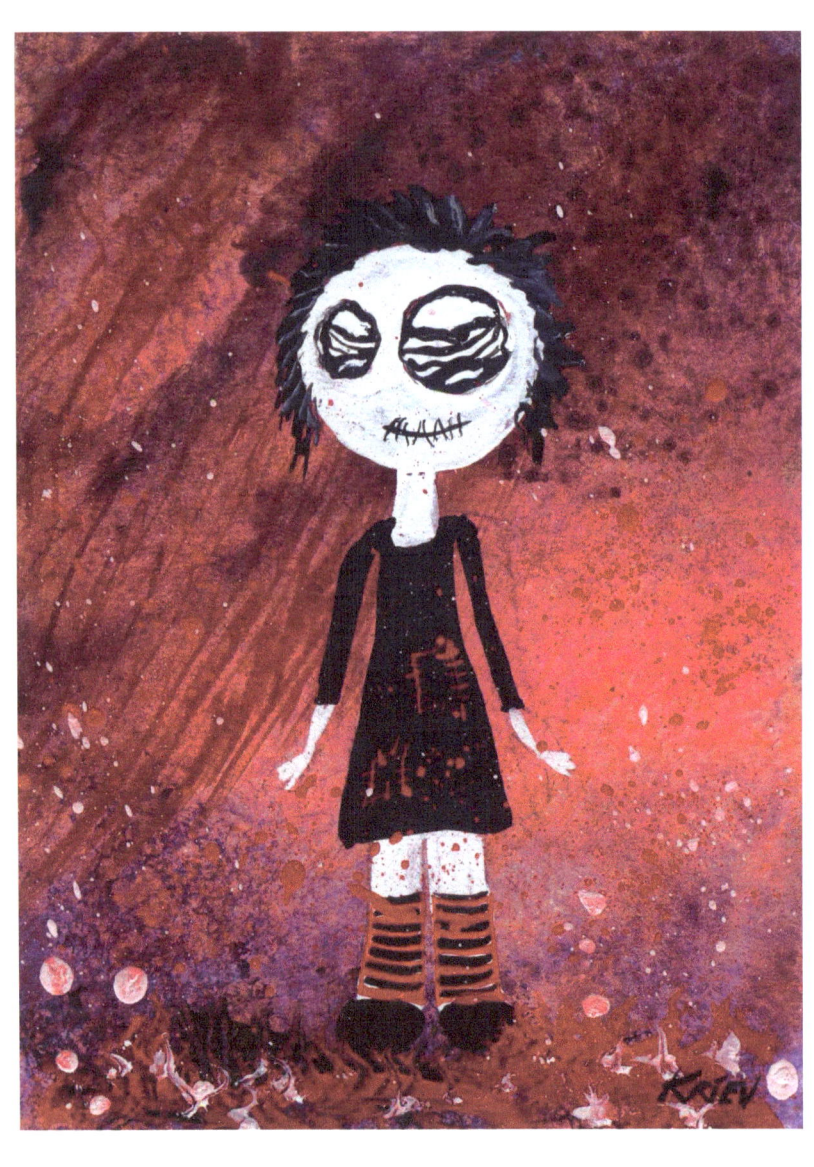

Rouge et Noir

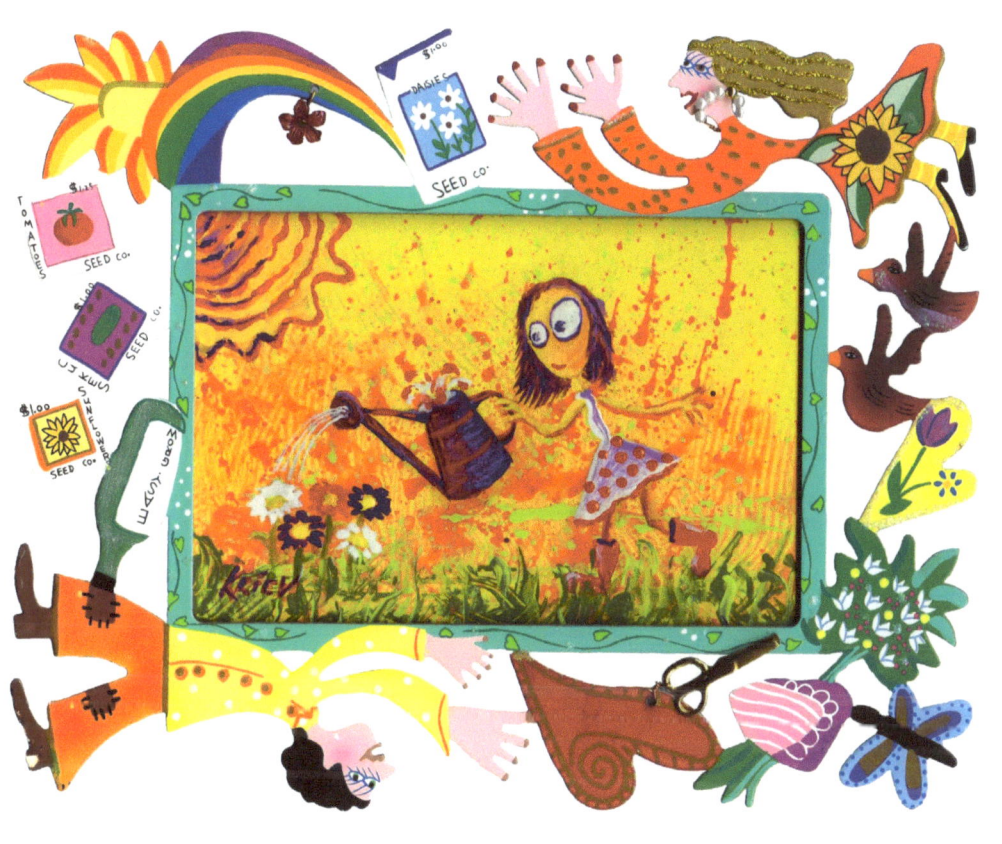

Spring Has Sprung

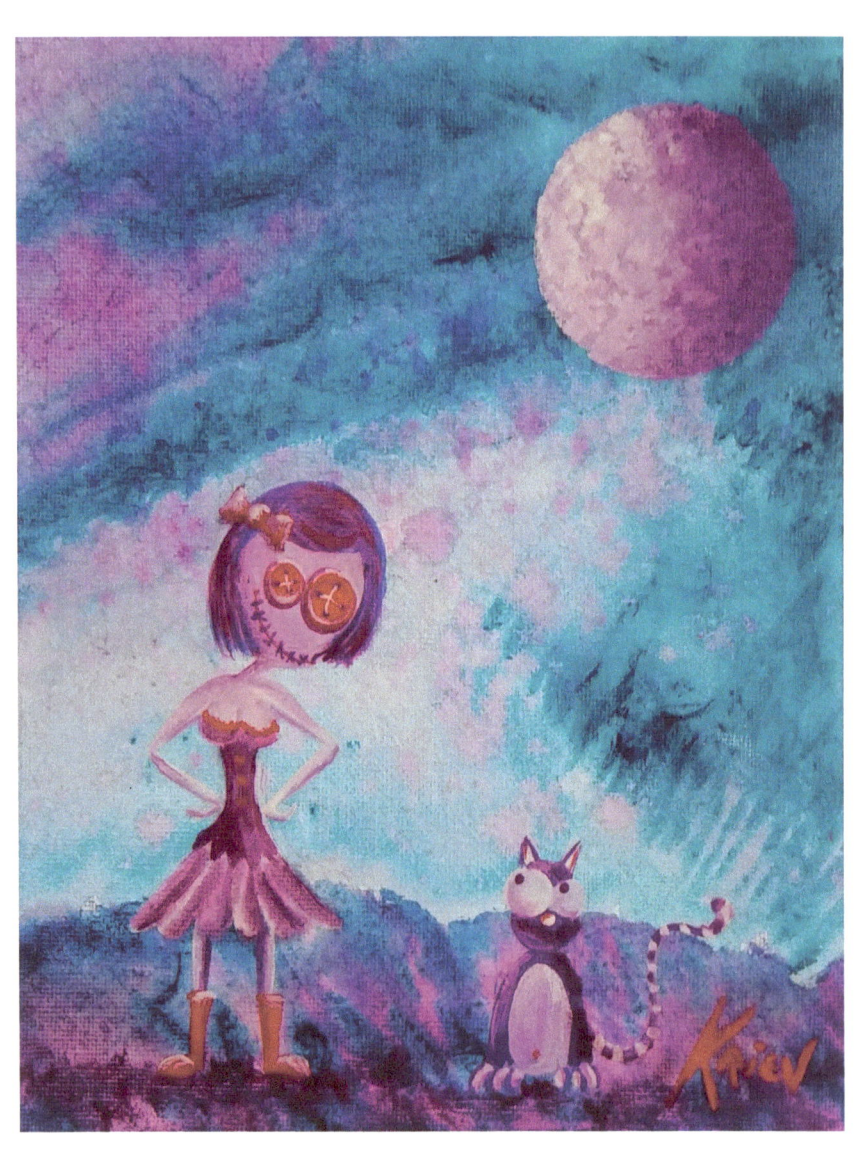

Bad Kitty!

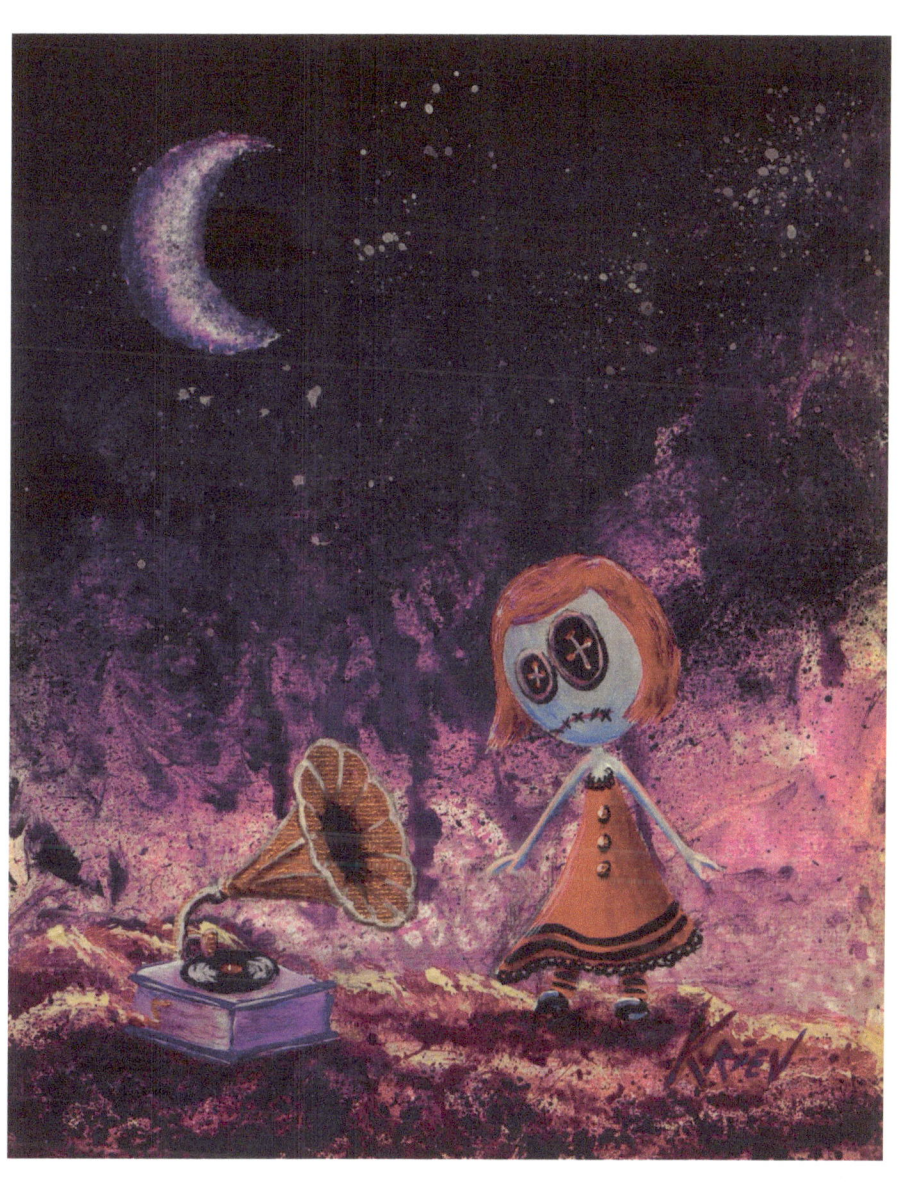

Musique Triste

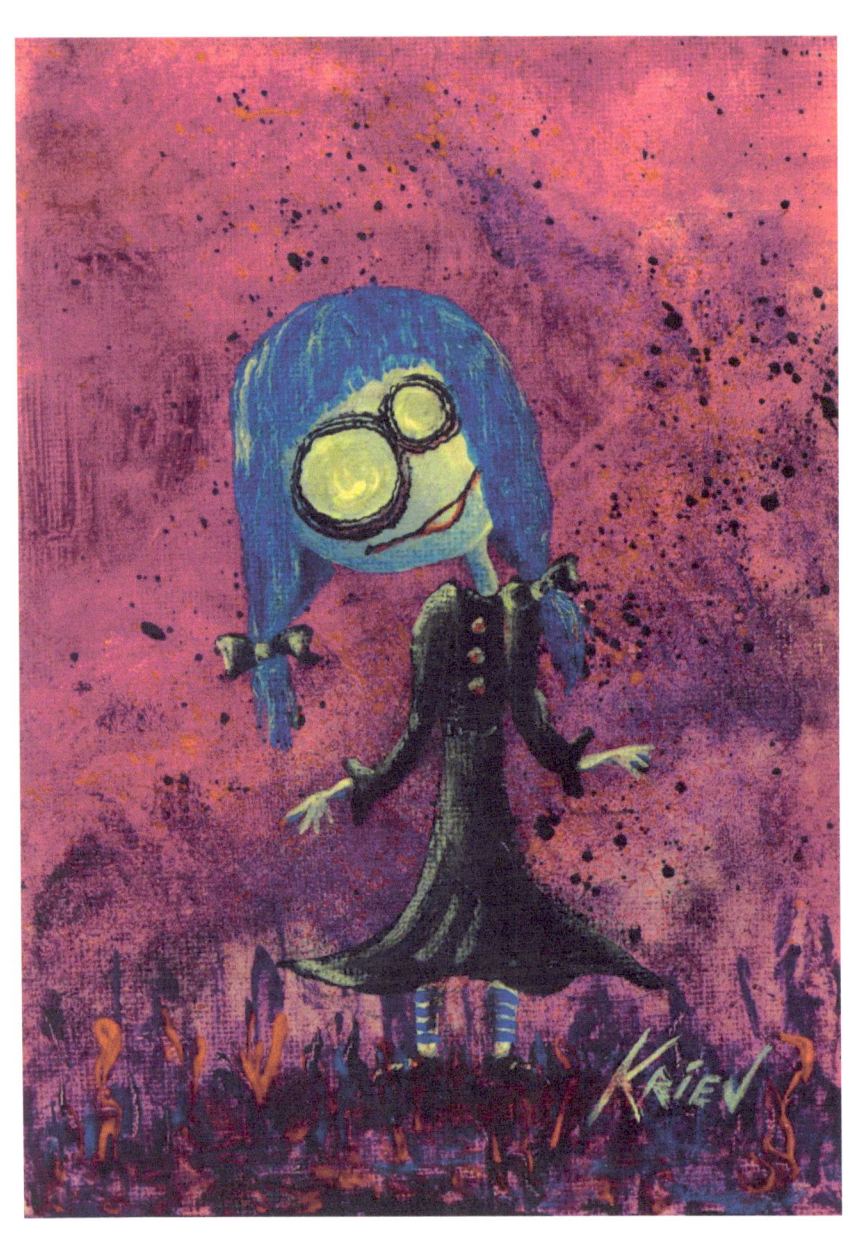

Little Blue

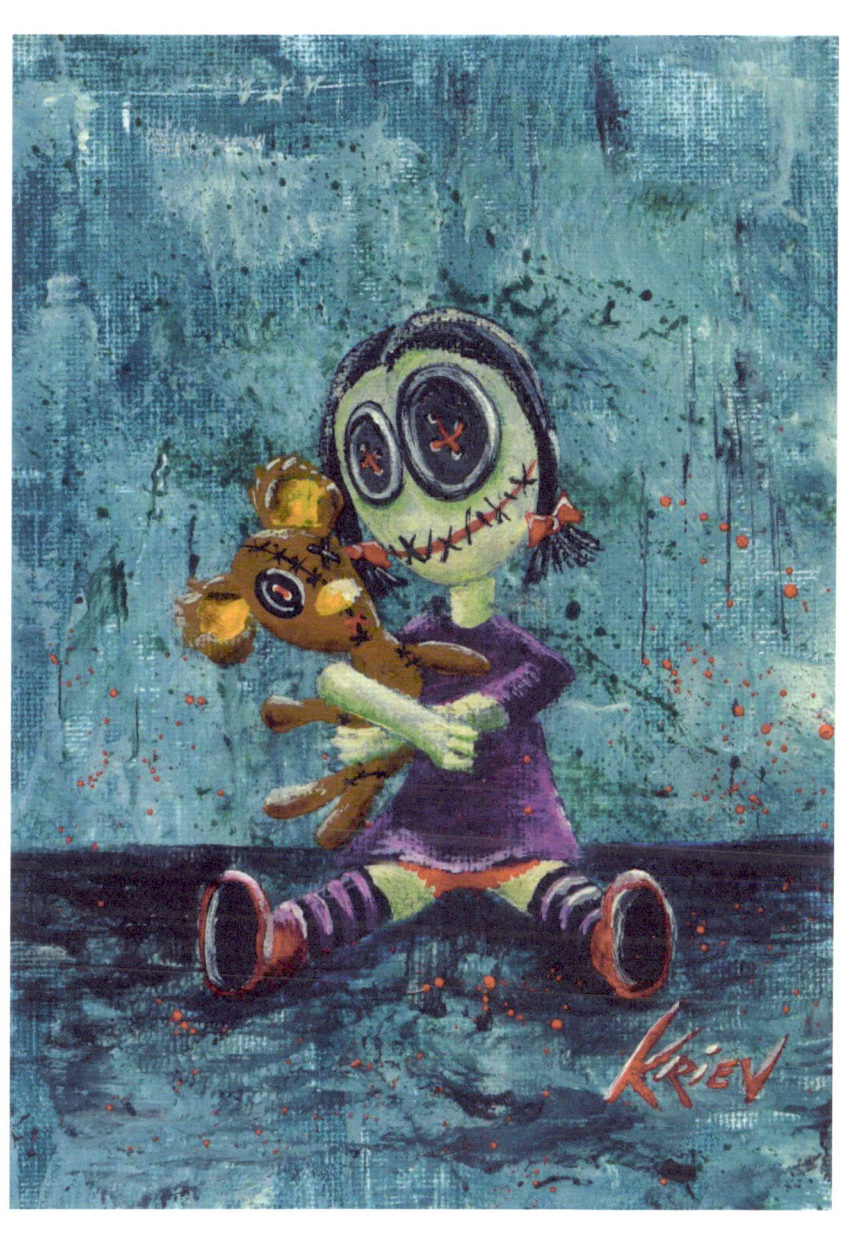

Brunus Edwardii

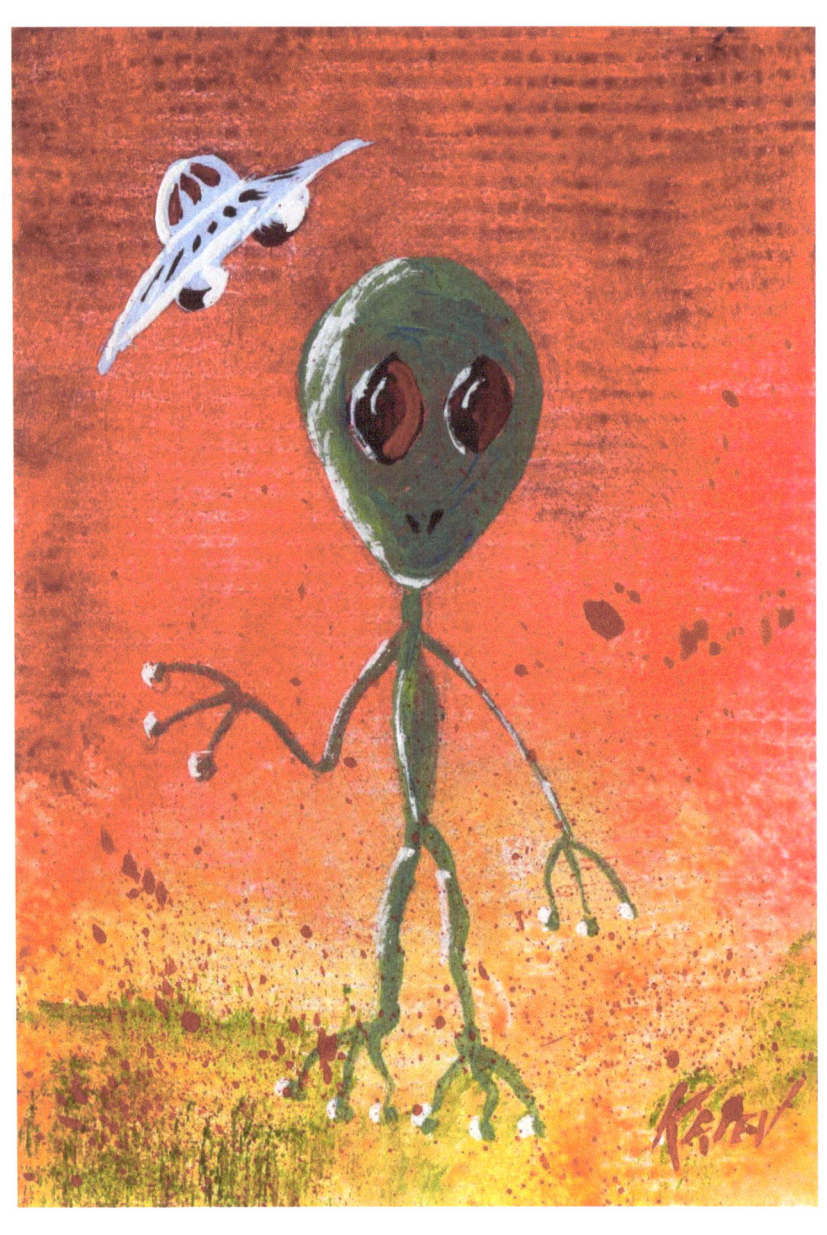

E.B.E.

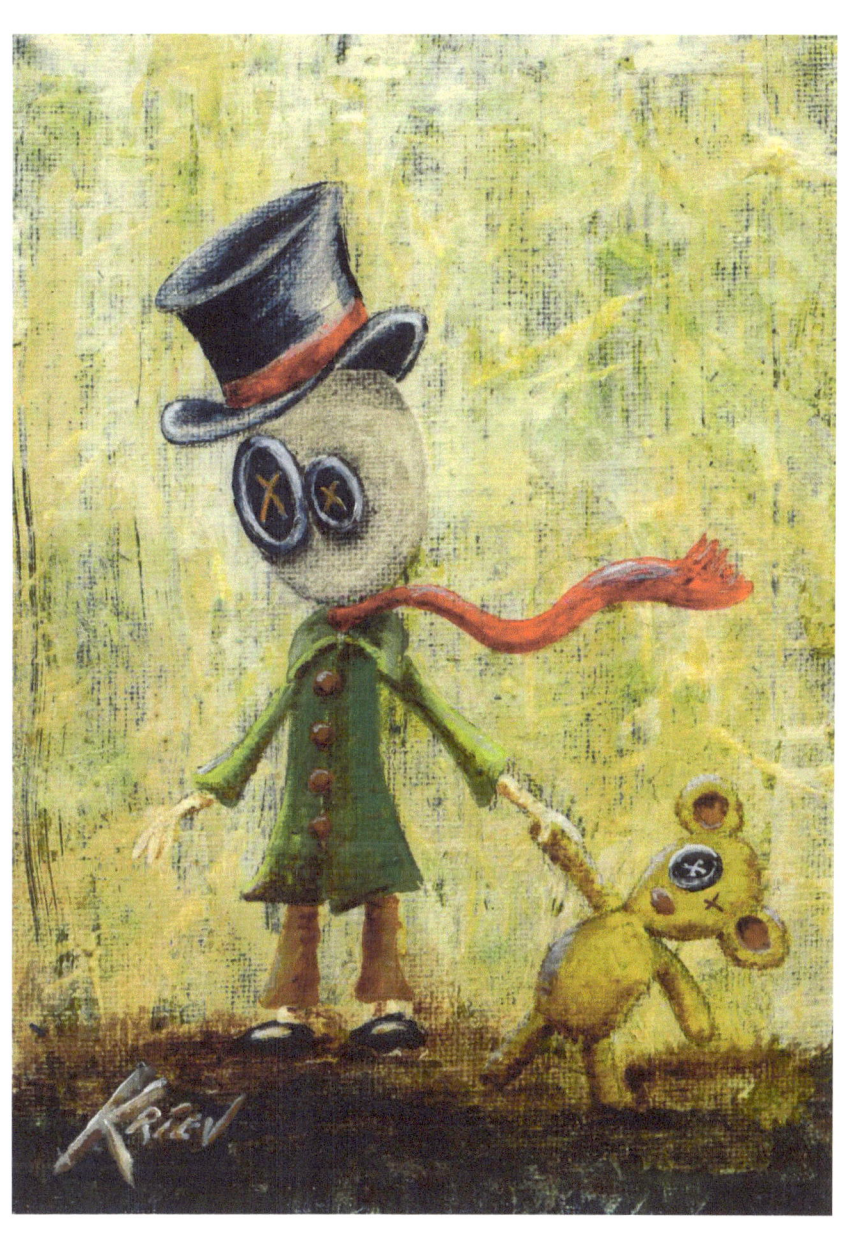

Teddy Doesn't Wanna Go

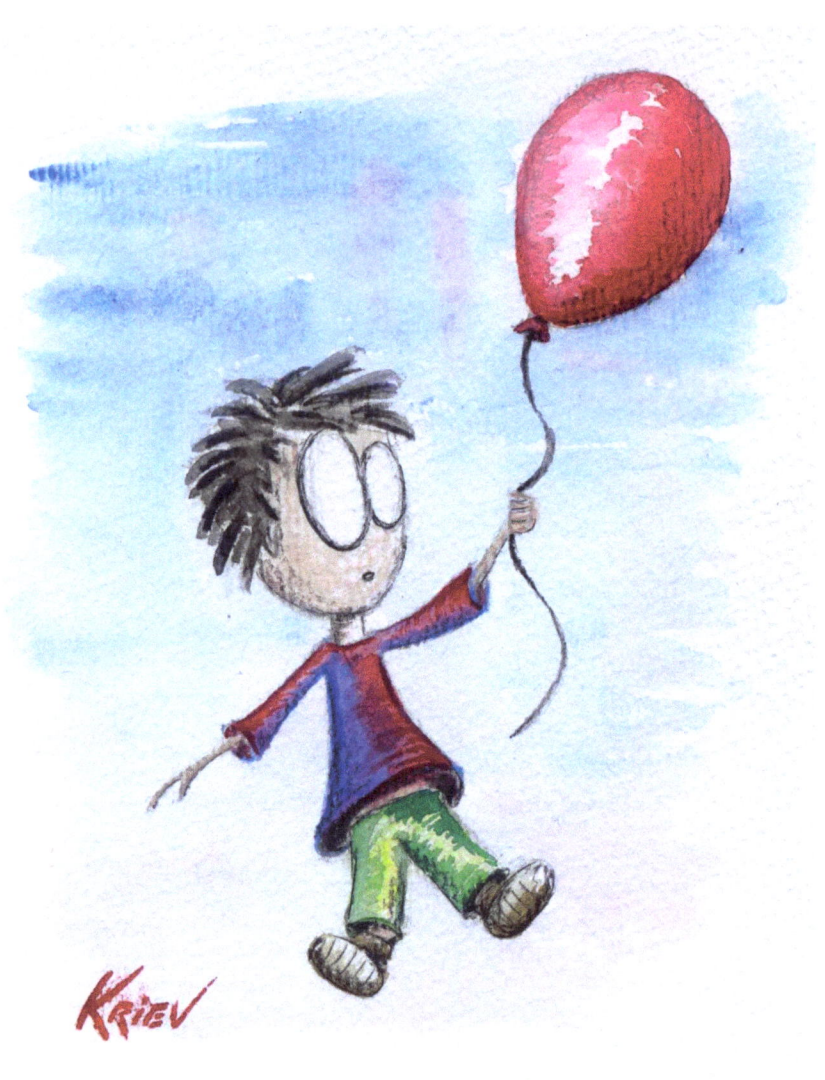

Balloon Boy

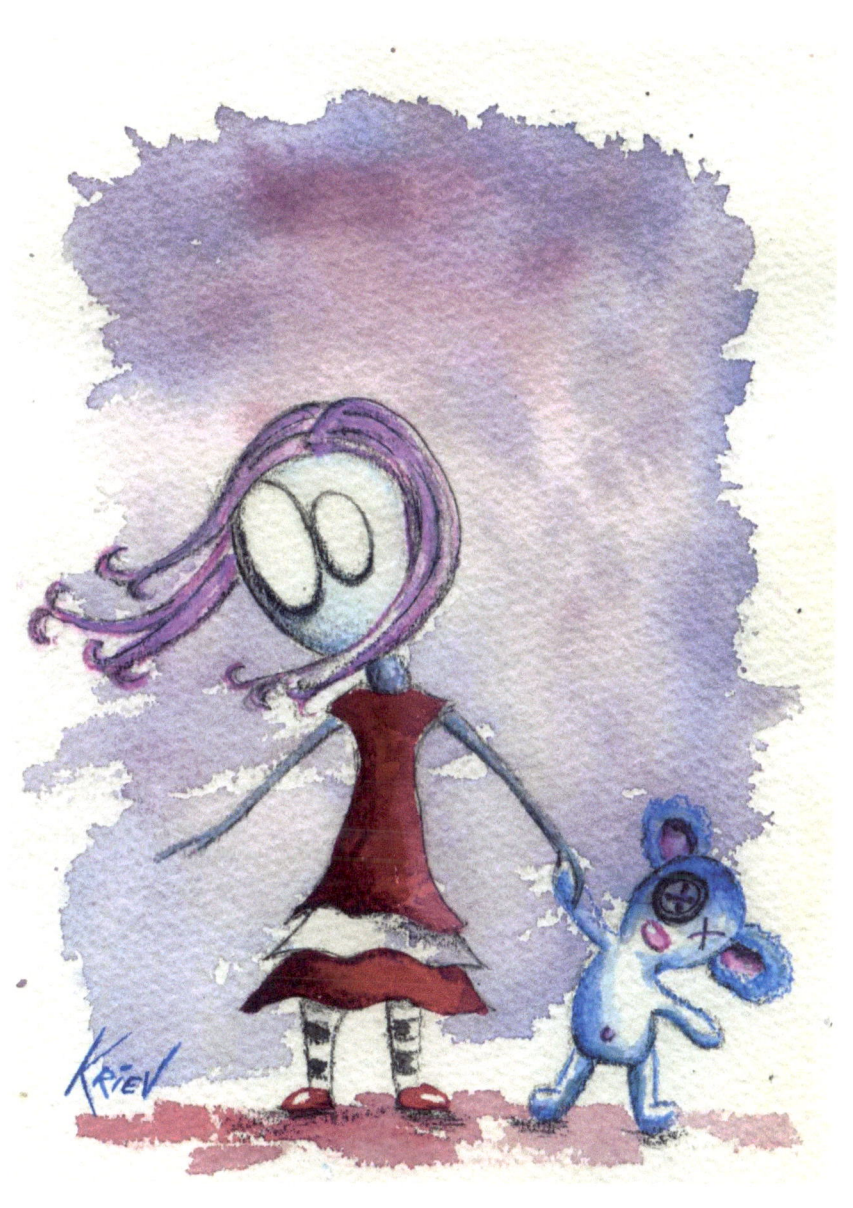

Blue Friend

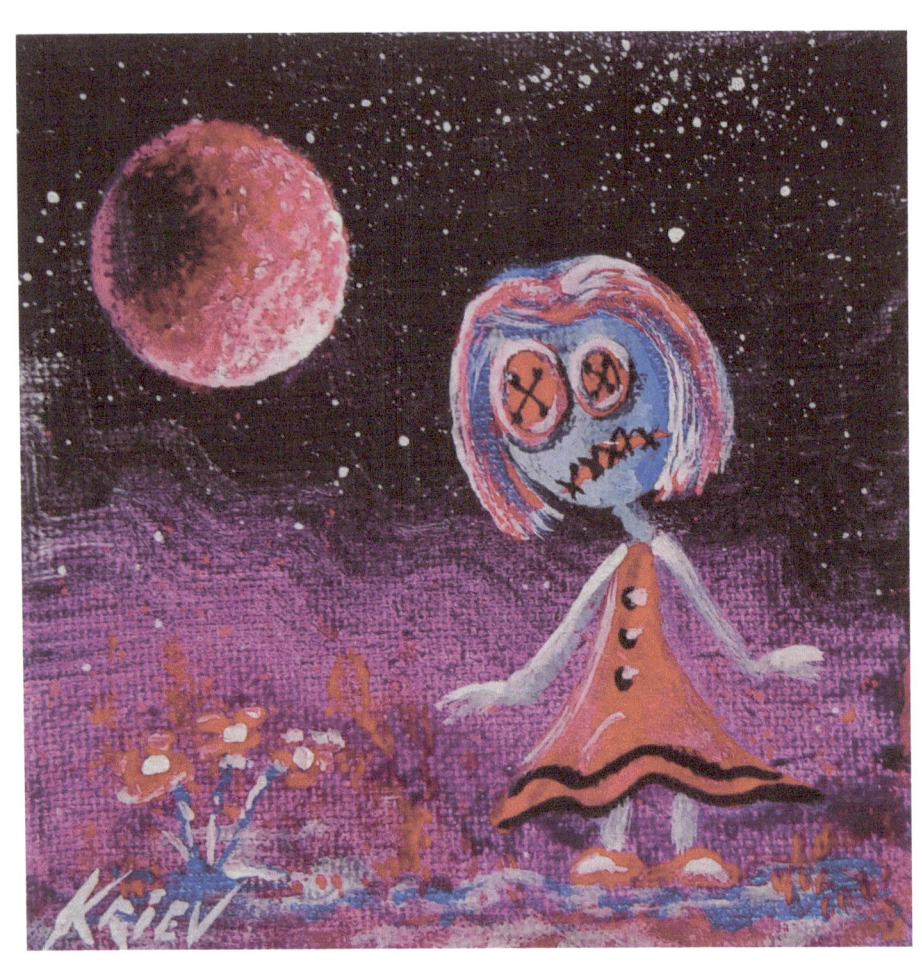

Night Flower

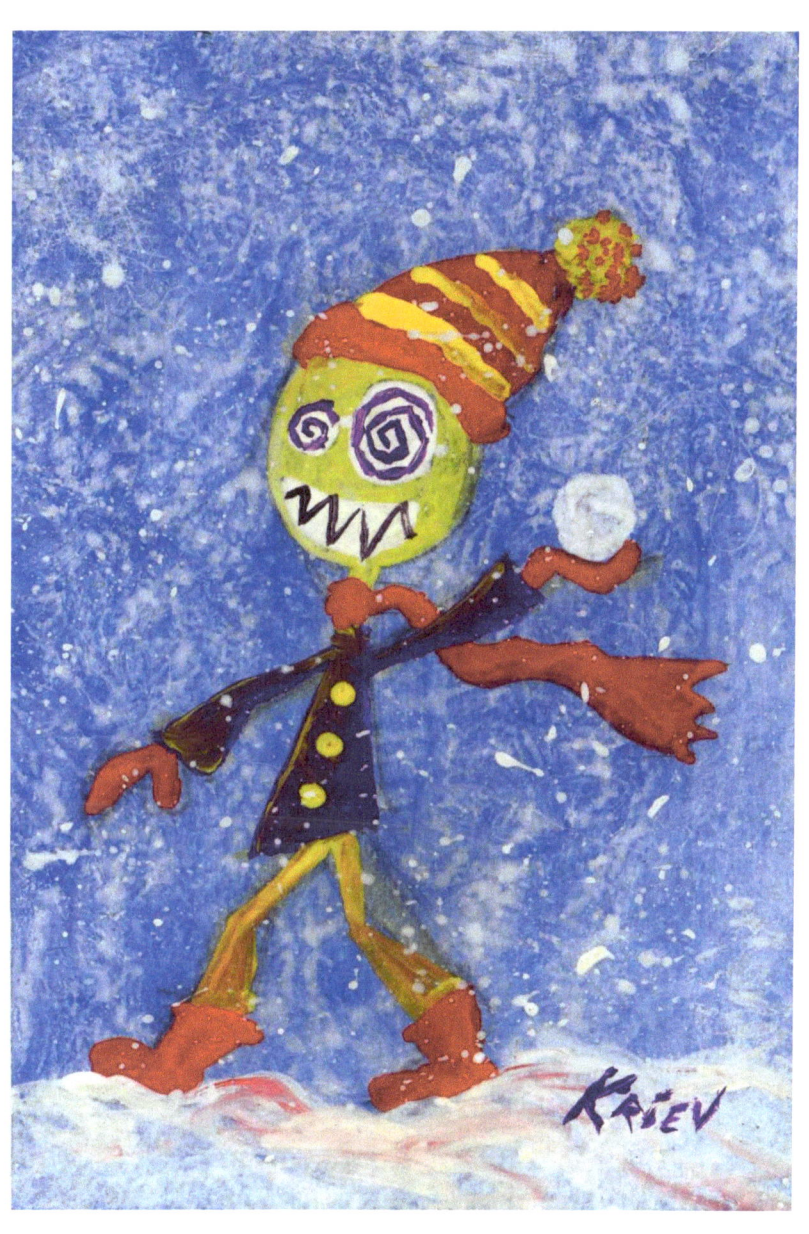

Snow Fight

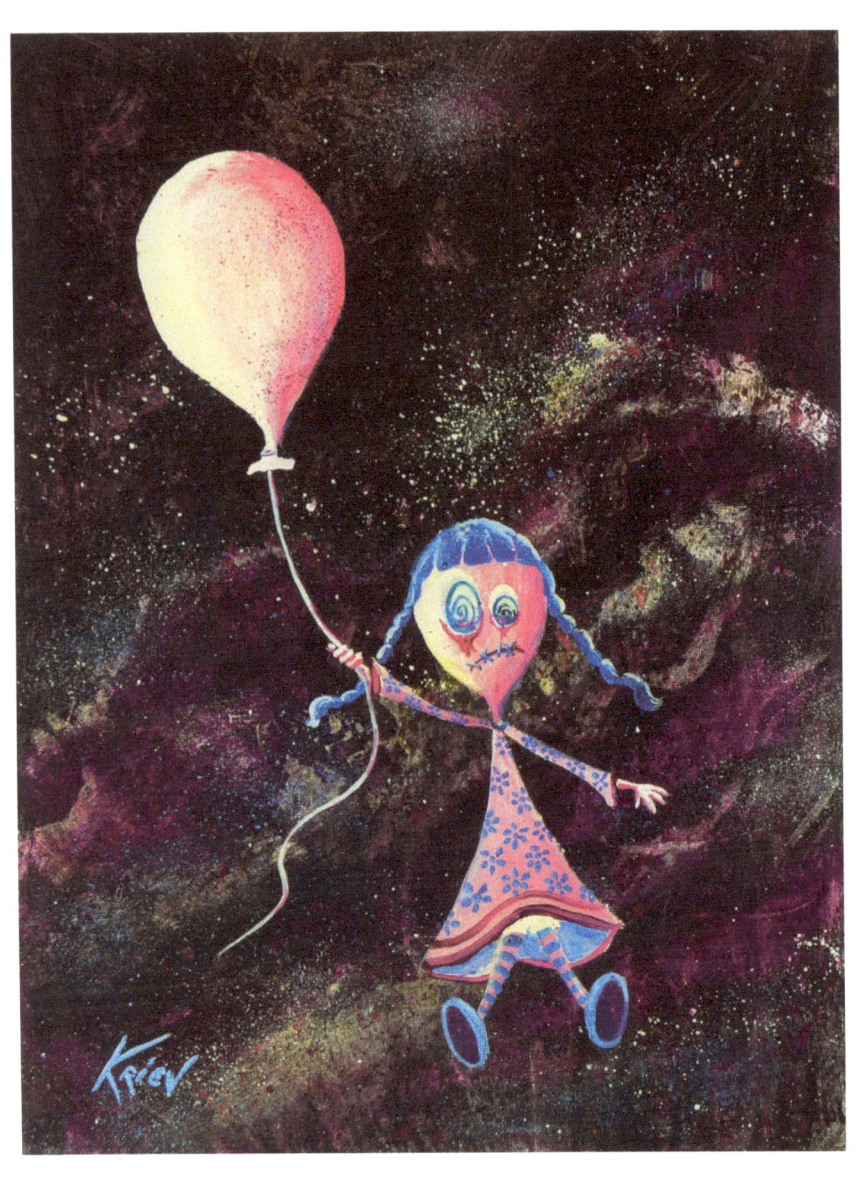

Up And Away

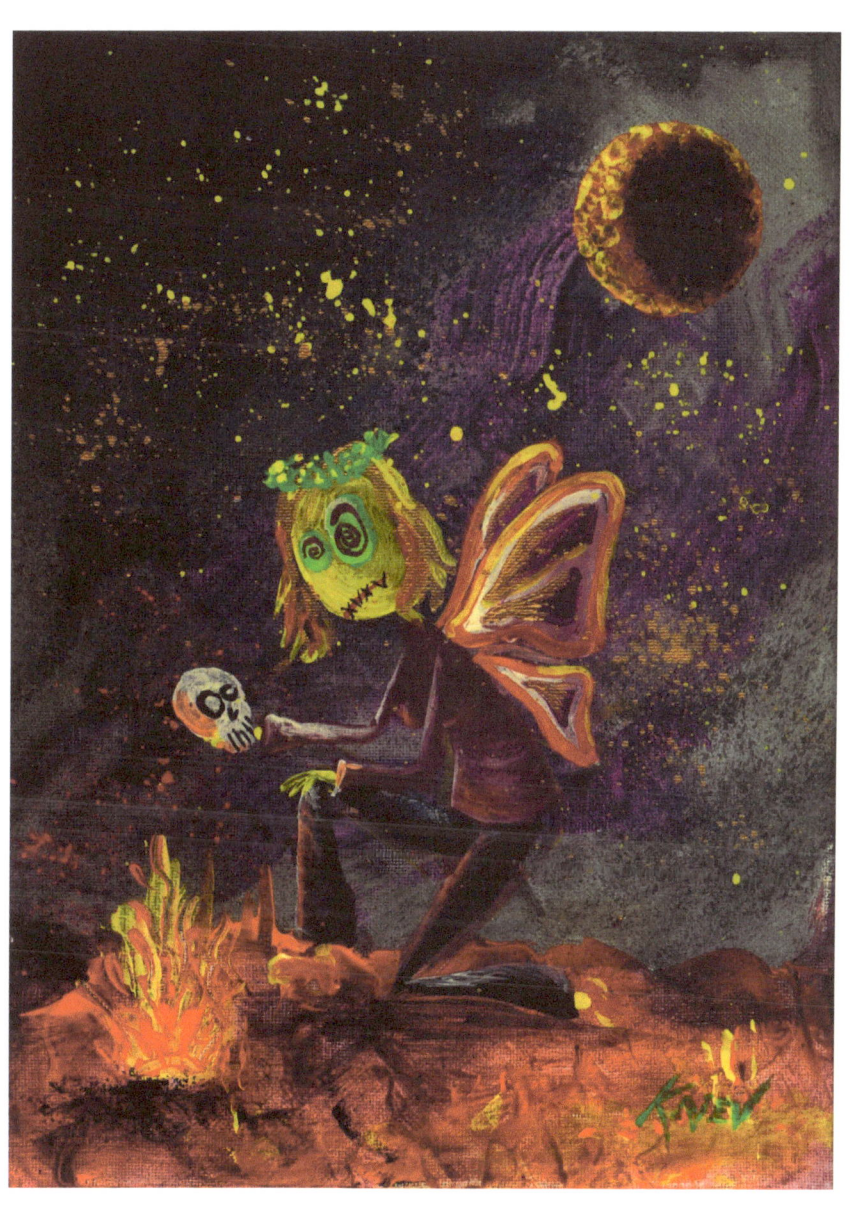

Night Faerie

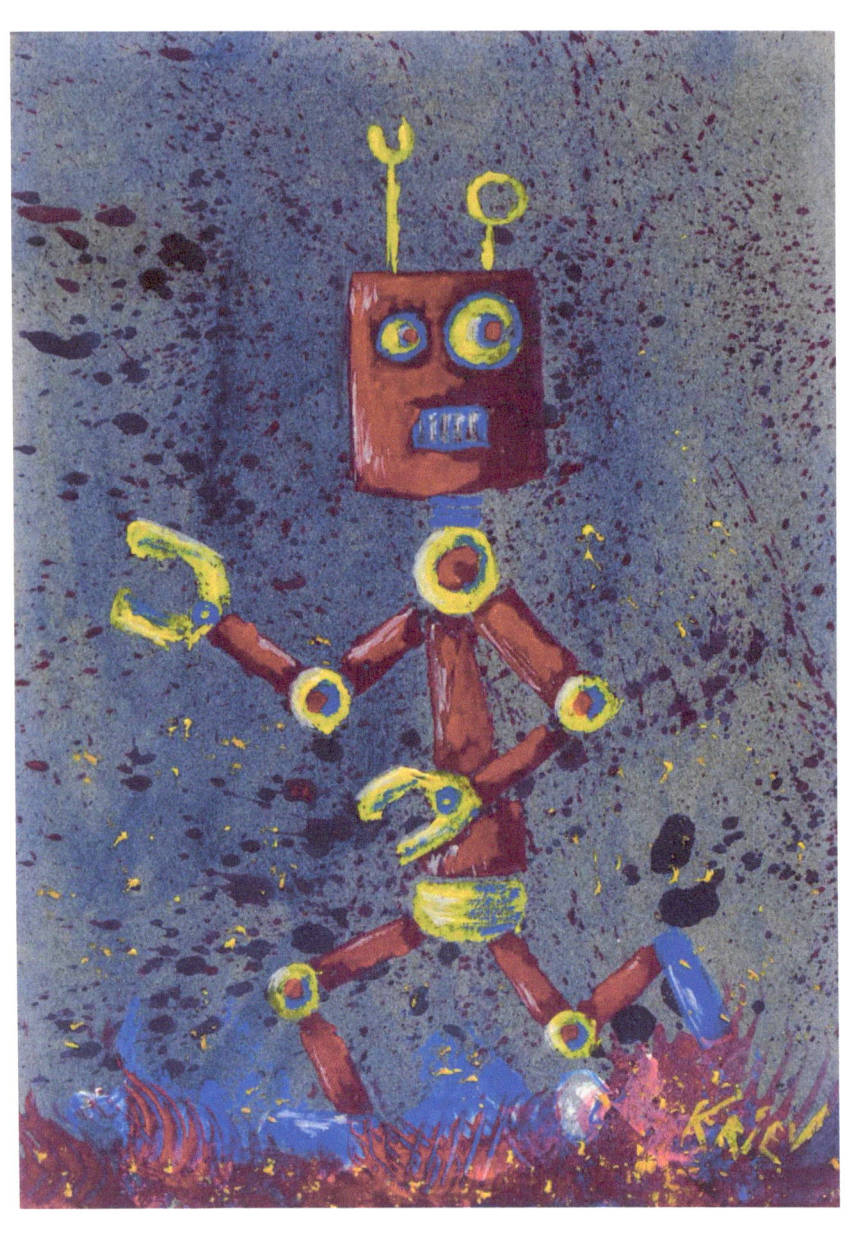

Run Robot Run

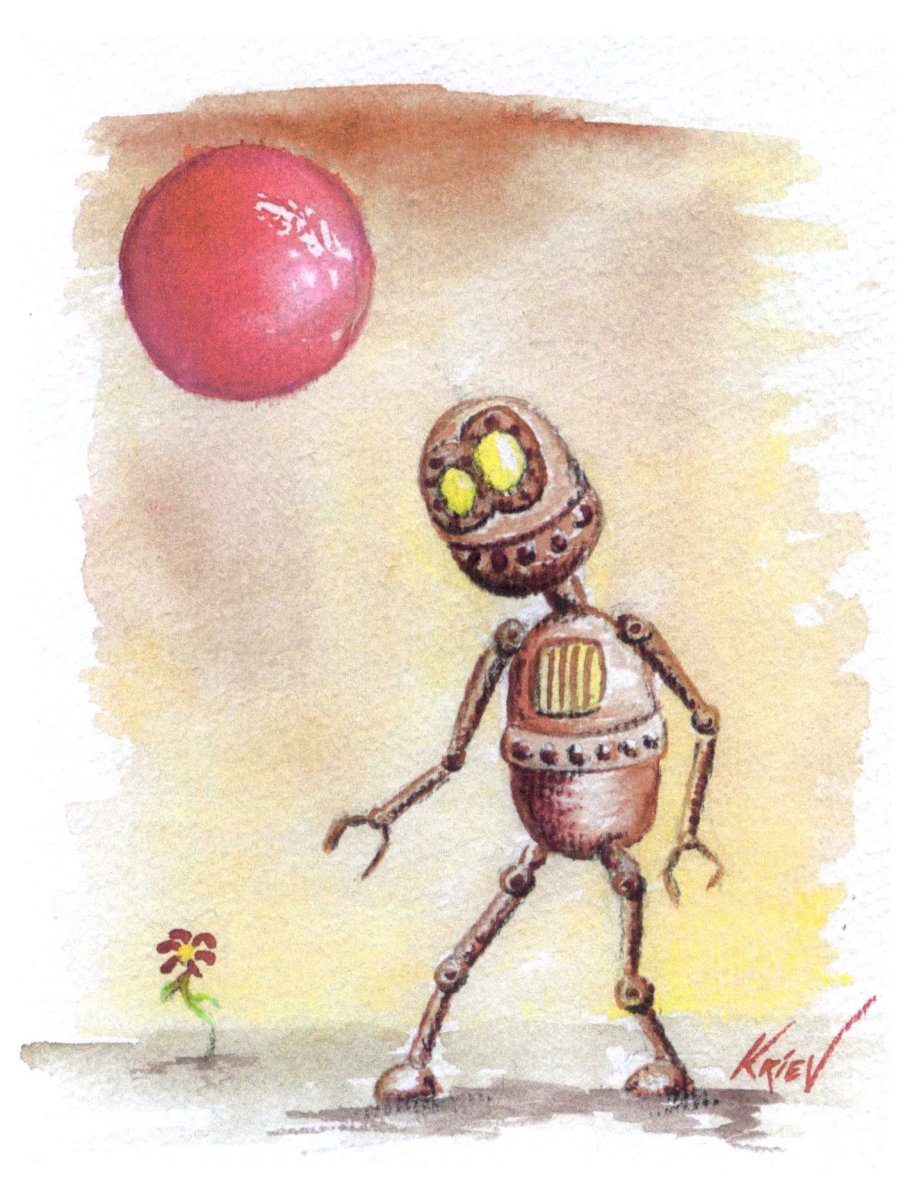

Steampunk Robot

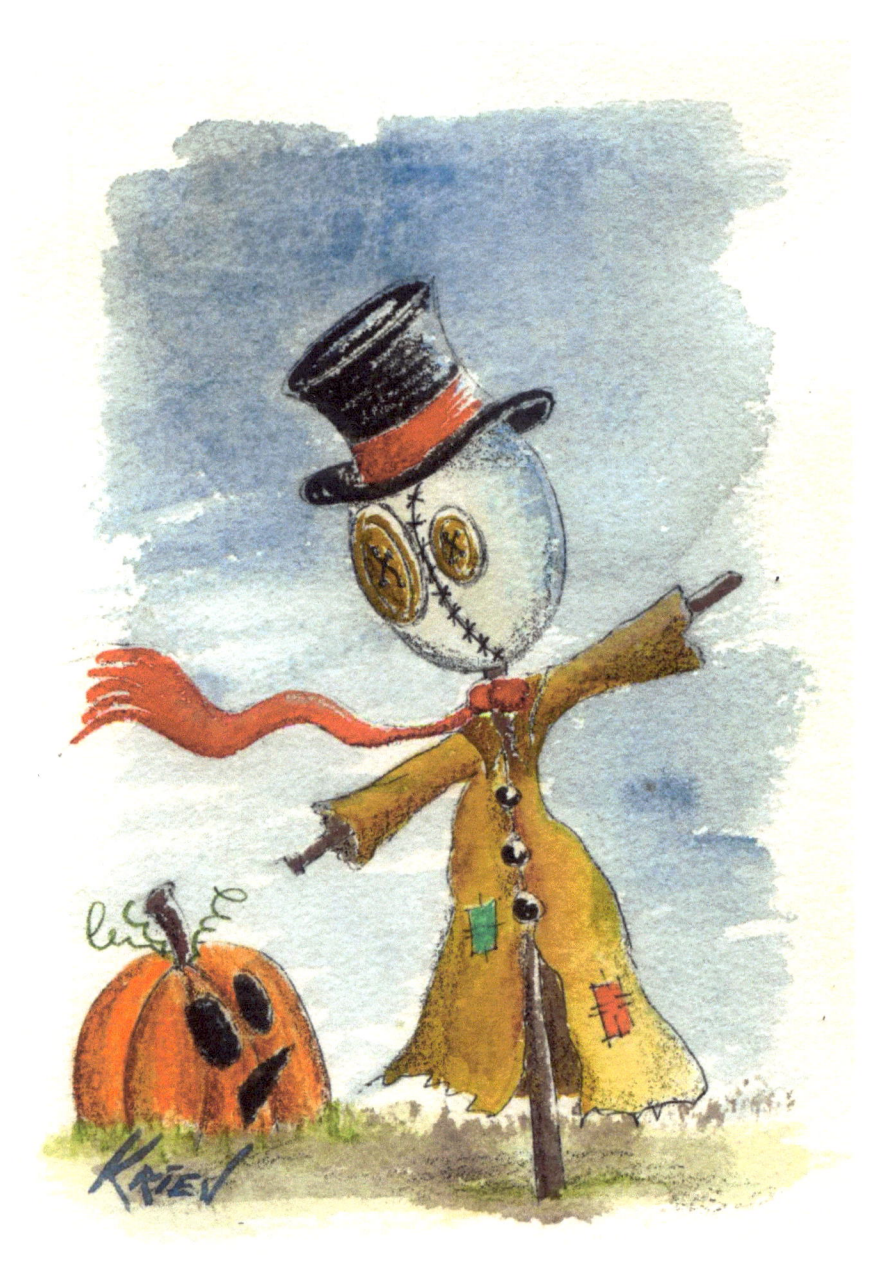

Autumn Conversation

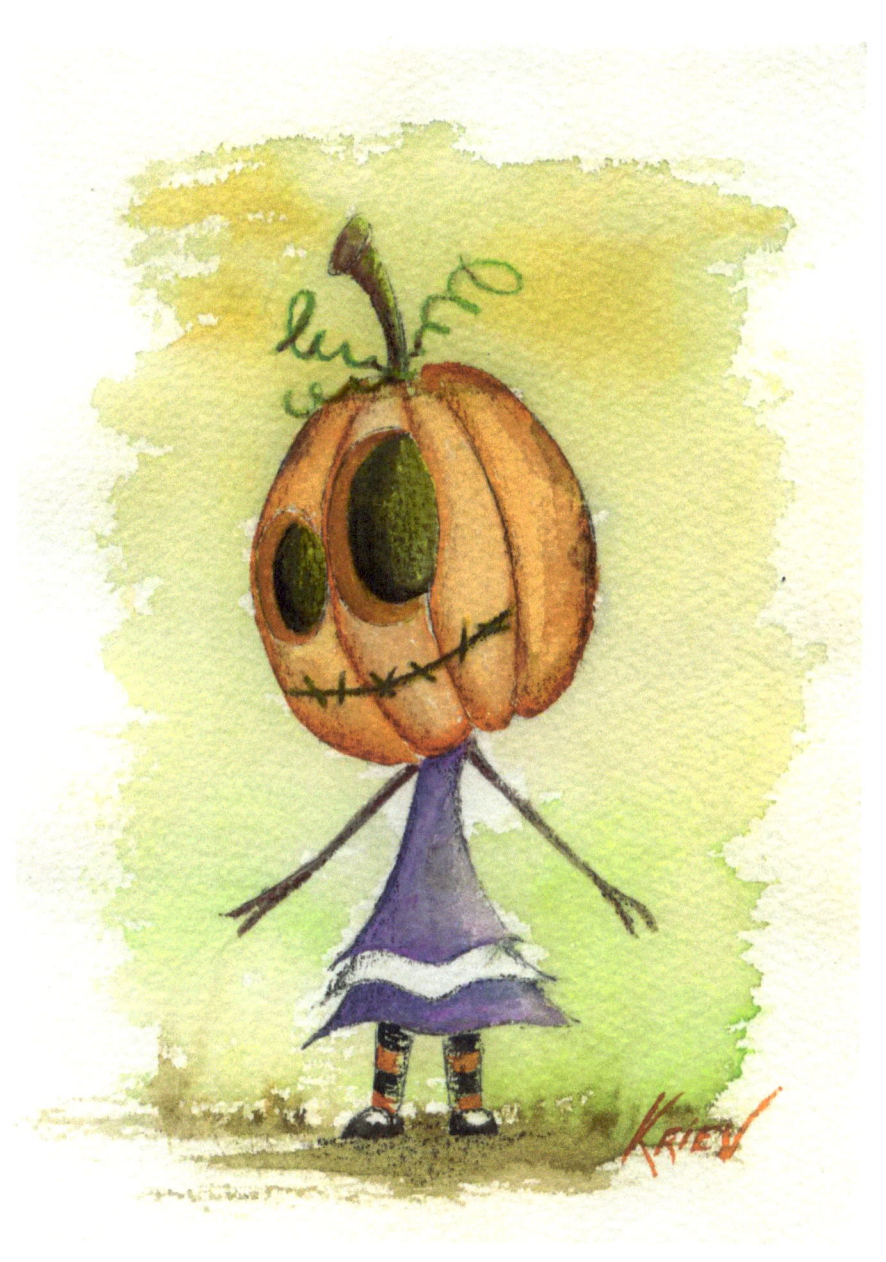

Citrouille Girl

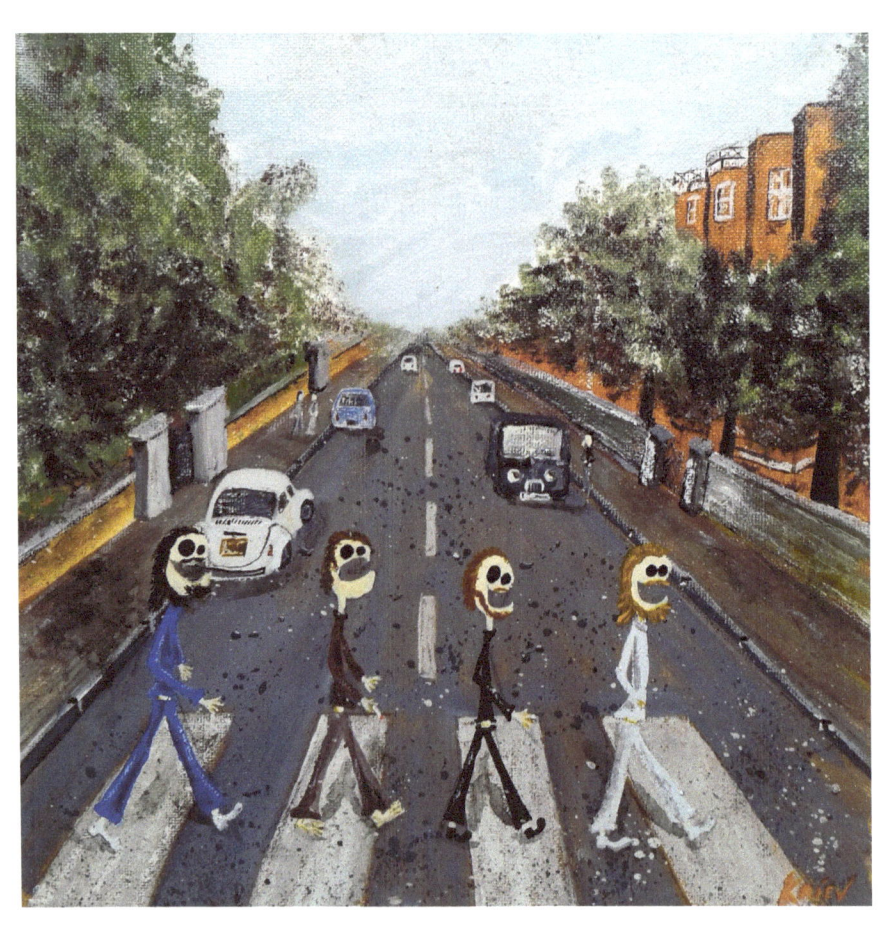

Zombie Road

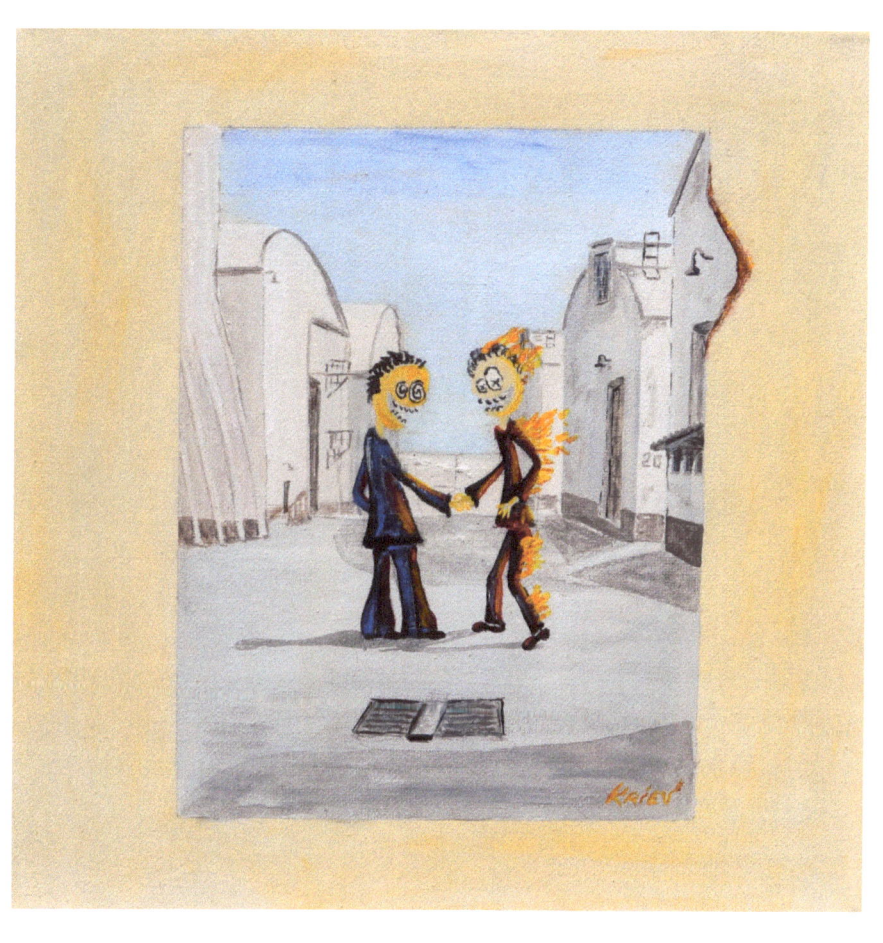

Wish You Were Hereafter

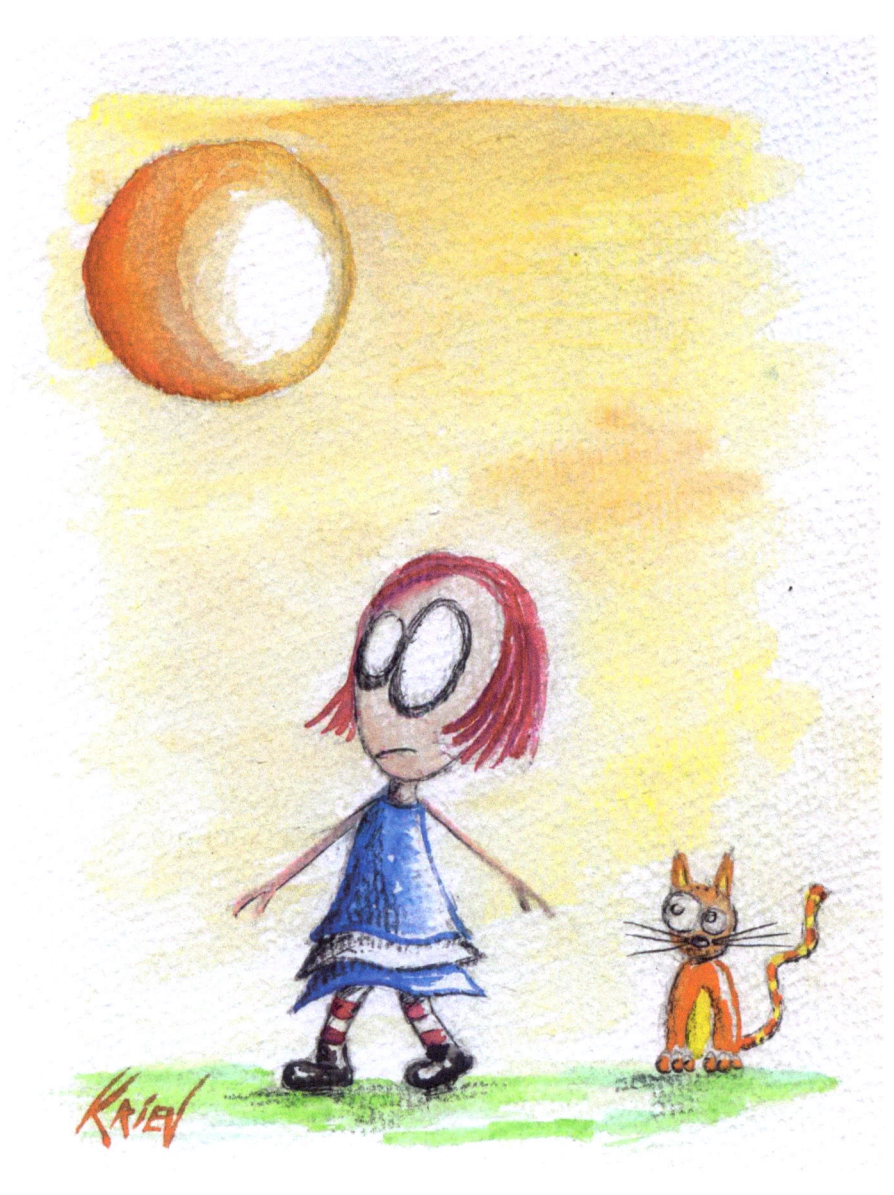

Meow!

www.ingramcontent.com/pod-product-compliance
Lightning Source LLC
Chambersburg PA
CBHW041945240526
45473CB00033B/615